THE TRICK IS IN THE TRAINING

THE TRICK
IS IN THE
TRAINING

25 Fun Tricks to Teach Your Dog

Stephanie J. Taunton and Cheryl S. Smith

BARRON'S

Stephanie J. Taunton is training director and owner of Bow Wow
Productions, an animal training facility for the film industry.
She is a state-certified dog trainer and has many animal credits
to her name, including animals performing in feature films,
commercials, and print. She has a very large variety of trained
animals at her facility in Northern California.

Cheryl S. Smith is an award-winning pet writer, with articles in
nearly all of the major pet magazines, and a variety of books
in print. She is a columnist for the newsletter of the Dog Writers'
Association of America and secretary of the Cat Writers' Association. She also writes for the stage, television, and movies, and
trains her own dogs, sheep, and chickens.

Copyright © 1998 by Stephanie J. Taunton and Cheryl S. Smith

All photographs by Ron Kimball Studios
Illustrations by Judith L. Winthrop

All inquiries should be addressed to:
Barron's Educational Series, Inc.
250 Wireless Boulevard
Hauppauge, NY 11788
http://www.barronseduc.com

International Standard Book No. 0-7641-0492-6

Library of Congress Catalog Card No. 97-34493

Library of Congress Cataloging-in-Publication Data

Taunton, Stephanie J.
    The trick is in the training : 25 fun tricks to teach your dog /
  Stephanie J. Taunton and Cheryl S. Smith.
        p.   cm.
      ISBN 0-7641-0492-6
      1. Dogs—Training.   I. Smith, Cheryl S.   II. Title.
  SF431.T385   1998
  636.7'0888—dc21   97-34493
                                                           CIP

Printed in Hong Kong/China
10 9 8 7

CONTENTS

ACKNOWLEDGMENTS

The authors would like to thank all the dog owners that allowed their dogs to participate in the book: Tiki – Dori Fontaine, Sasha – Jen Holz, Sarge – Wendy and Jerry Reagan, Juanita – Blythe Verstrepen, Ranger – Anna LaFrom, Misty (Beagle) – Dawn-Marie Shoffner, Toby – Michelle Borchardt, Misty (Golden Retriever) – Rosanne Sax and Ken Piccolino, Doogie – Alycia Hinton, Shady – Linda Penney, Sasha (cattle dog) – Lorri Scheller, Buster – Carolyn Ouellette, Cubby – Dana Sansing, and Tessa – Larry Thomas. Dogs owned by Stephanie Taunton: Sunday, Peaches, Molly, Sheppie, Jessie, Dutch, Boone, Magic, McGee, Kelly, Touché, and Marquis the cat. Our thanks also to the trainers that handled the dogs—Sapir Weiss, Donna Johns, Jill Jensky, and Julie Hersk; and to Jan Nelson for helping to show how these behaviors can be used in a practical manner for the physically challenged; Ron Kimball for his patience and photographic expertise; Judy Winthrop for her suggestions and illustrations; Javier Flores for playing the bad guy; Kim Verstrepen for her input and help; and Serling and Diamond for getting Cheryl Smith involved with Stephanie Taunton.

To my parents, who taught me to find solutions to my own problems, and to my dogs, who forced me to be creative in seeking those solutions.

— Cheryl S. Smith

To Sapir Weiss, my mentor, who has helped me throughout my career with guidance and support.

— Stephanie J. Taunton

FOREWORD

When Stephanie first asked if I would take the pictures to illustrate her book, I was delighted. Over the past ten years I've watched Stephanie grow from a rookie with a knack for handling animals to one of the top animal trainers in the country.

We have worked together on greeting cards, calendars, posters, and advertising projects. Stephanie has taught pigs to dance and frogs to ride miniature motorcycles. During all our many photographic sessions she has demonstrated innovation, understanding of how to motivate animals of all sorts, and a never-say-die attitude.

Stephanie's own dogs are mostly rescued from animal shelters, purebred groups, or even straight off the streets. They are chosen to be photogenic, and range in intelligence from rather slow to extremely quick. Most were no longer puppies when they joined up with Stephanie. It doesn't matter—she trains them all—and consistently succeeds at assignments where other trainers fail. Whether it's miniature puzzles or big-budget motion pictures, she gets the job done.

The objective of this book is to share with the reader some of the techniques used by Stephanie's Bow Wow Productions. The techniques are shown clearly and are easy to understand. Learning some of the tricks of animal acting should be fun and interesting for both the dog and the dog owner. What a great way to develop a more intimate relationship with your dog!

Ron Kimball
Ron Kimball Studios
Mountain View, California

CHAPTER 1
DOING WHAT COMES NATURALLY

As the title of the book indicates, what we will discuss here is how to teach what are usually thought of as "tricks" to your dog. That word "tricks" is misleading. All of the exercises you and your dog will learn here are based on natural behaviors or extensions of natural behaviors. What we will do is teach you how to train your dog to perform them on command. Rather than "trick training," we call this "animal acting." (This same strategy of training works equally well for many animals besides dogs. You can use these lessons to train your cat, horse, potbellied pig, or whatever—as long as your pet is food motivated, you can teach it some acting. Keep any physical limitations in mind—pigs are NOT good candidates for sitting up, and horses just WON'T crawl like a dog.)

Dogs act on their own just fine. If you're sitting and eating a nice juicy cheeseburger and your dog is watching, you can surely read the message in his pathetic yearning eyes. Or jingle your car keys or pick up a leash and watch an exhibit of pure unadulterated joy. Using your dog's natural abilities and adding some training, you can have a dog that will look ashamed (Head Down, p.34), excited (Circle Left/Circle Right, p.50), or apprehensive (Where's Your Nose?, p.30) on command.

You will also see your dog shine with new enthusiasm and intelligence. These are animals bred to hunt, track, herd, guard, kill vermin, and pull carts. We rarely use these natural abilities. Animal acting will tap into these hidden talents and give your dog a more fulfilling station in life.

Marquee

Here is an example of a natural behavior. Dogs are always putting their front paws on all sorts of things and getting in all kinds of trouble for it. Ask any trainer of basic obedience classes what complaint he or she hears most, and you're sure to be told "jumping up." Now you can put that behavior to good use AND control when it happens. Jumping up will become "Feet up," with you choosing the target (instructions are in Chapter 7).

"Feet up" can pose a dog beautifully for photographs, whether you're taking some snapshots for your own pleasure or a professional has decided your canine is calendar material. It's a very helpful behavior in pet therapy work—having a dog that will carefully put her feet

Sunday, mixed breed

up on the side of a bed or the arm of a wheelchair helps patients with limited mobility give a pat or receive a kiss (another natural behavior easy to put on cue—see Chapter 10).

"Feet up" is also very useful when you *do* want the dog to get up on something. Most dogs too heavy to pick up easily can reach a grooming table or the tailgate of a pickup truck with their front feet. You can then just boost their back end up onto the table or into the truck, saving wear and tear on your back. The two-year-old that boings into a truck with scarcely a thought may be glad of a boost in eight or nine years. You'll be glad you taught "Feet up."

Some of the behaviors included here are used in professional work all the time. Watch all those dog-inhabited commercials, TV shows, and movies and you'll probably see "Head down," "Sit up," and "Speak" more than once. If you're a "stage master" with acting aspirations for your best friend, having a repertoire of these behaviors on cue will certainly put you ahead of the pack. Other behaviors are rarely called for in professional circles, but may be a hit in convalescent hospital activity rooms or at county fair animal talent competitions. All are easily accomplished by the average dog and handler.

Tiki, mixed breed

Practicing these behaviors should be FUN for you and your dog. Don't get all grim and uptight about it. Some take longer than others to perfect, and some dogs are better at one thing than another. Stars are made, not born. All dogs in good physical and mental condition should eventually master all of them. (And, not to lay all the blame on the dog, some handlers are naturally talented and some are just a bit klutzy. Follow the tips about timing and problem solving included with each of the behavior write-ups and you'll do fine.)

Animal acting creates a great bond between you and your dog. Especially if yours is not an active lifestyle, it will give you both a workout.

One important reminder—reward behaviors only when you have requested them or you will soon find your dog playing you like a finely tuned fiddle, cashing in on cookies whenever he wants. It may be really hard to ignore your dog when he places himself between you and the TV, looks you straight in the eye, and sits up and waves, but *you're* supposed to be the one in charge.

Odds are that your dog won't get a chance to show her stuff on camera or in print, though you never know—Chapter 3 gives some information on the world of the professional. But you WILL both have some fun, learn new things, and at the very least have something to show off on your walks in the park.

Sasha, mixed breed

CHAPTER 2
SO WHAT'S MY MOTIVATION?

If you've been involved in any obedience training, you may have discovered that there are two popular modes of training: with food and with corrections. Food training is based on luring the dog into position and rewarding him with the food. Correction training is based on placing the dog into position and rewarding with praise. The corrections, typically a jerk on a training collar, are used for nonresponses or incorrect behavior. Check out some obedience seminars or read some obedience periodicals and you'll encounter terms such as "lure" and "shaping" and theories of "drives" and "negative reinforcers." But this is *not* a training theory book, and we won't get into all of that here. All you need to do is follow the instructions for each of the behaviors.

In animal acting, we use a little of everything, whatever we need to elicit a particular behavior. But our most important tools are food rewards and praise, with some physical manipulation thrown in.

So, you need to know what best motivates your dog. Some dogs have strong food motivation, others have a strong prey drive, some will have both. Food motivation tends to be the easiest training method. Dogs with strong prey drives like to play with balls and squeaky toys, but have to be in the mood to do so. Dogs with strong food drives tend to act ravenous all the time and are always interested in eating. If your dog likes both food and toys, you can try switching from one to the other when training a particular behavior to see which gets a better response.

Animal acting does use a substantial amount of food, especially when teaching new behaviors. If you have a dog that gains weight by merely sniffing food, you will need to plan how to avoid ending up with a well-trained but seriously obese dog.

Sarge, Bulldog

If the dog eats anything any time, the simplest strategy is to use some of the dog's regular kibble as your training treat. Don't forget to deduct that amount from the dog's dinner bowl. You can even measure the dog's ration into the bowl in the morning, dip into it for your training sessions through the day, and feed whatever is left for dinner. Leaving food down for the dog all day will lower his food motivation and make it difficult to train some behaviors. A hungry dog is a motivated dog.

Some dogs just are not excited about their regular old kibble as a treat. There are literally hundreds of dog treats to choose from. You need to find a treat that your dog finds exciting, that can be eaten quickly, and that can be tossed over some distance to your dog. Tossing a treat keeps the dog at a distance waiting for the treat rather than moving toward you. A bait bag or fanny pack will give you a convenient accessible place to keep your treats while training.

The timing of your reward is extremely important, so much so that each set of behavior instructions in the book includes a quick section specifying when to give the dog the treat. Incorrect timing means you are not rewarding the correct action. If your dog sits up beautifully but your reward comes when her front feet are back on the ground, she may think the action you are after is a quick "Sit up, sit down" sequence. Always consider what you are rewarding. Associate the command with the action with the reward. The more dramatic you make your signals and body language, the better response you'll get from the dog. Now is not the time to be self-conscious.

As your dog becomes more accomplished at a behavior, you should offer food less often. If you continue to reward every performance, quality will gradually deteriorate. The dog will do as little as possible to receive the reward. Once a behavior is learned, you reward at random or choose only the best performances to reward. This sporadic payoff keeps the dog working to earn his reward. When your dog is proficient in many behaviors, ask him to perform several before he's rewarded with food.

And food is not the only reward. Your praise should be equally valuable to your dog. This is not likely to be the case if your praise consists of a monotone, "Good boy." Your praise needs to be genuine and enthusiastic. Here, too, you need to learn what motivates your dog. With a high-energy, totally keyed-in dog, a simple "Good dog" may be enough. But the average dog requires more. You may, in fact, need to use a high, squeaky voice, gyrate like a cheerleader, and behave in a way that makes you feel like a complete fool. This is your performance for your dog.

Learn what works best with your dog and use it to your advantage.

Hand signals can be difficult to describe or even show in photographs, as most of them are moving signals. They are based on the movements you make while teaching the dog a behavior. So the sweep of your hand up and back over the dog's head to lure him into a sit up becomes the same up and out

Juanita, Poodle mix

Sunday, mixed breed

hand movement used even when you are standing up and signalling a dog ten feet away once the behavior is learned. The signals shown here are fairly standard in the professional animal acting business and used by most of the handlers. But it is not important that you copy them exactly. You can use whatever works for you, as long as the dog can see a signal and recognize what it means.

While teaching a behavior, you use both a command and a rough version of a signal. Once the behavior is learned, you should be able to use a command alone, a signal alone, or both together. Your performance is often more impressive if you use just signals, as your audience may not even be aware that you are cuing the dog.

Try to pick three or four behaviors, each out of a different chapter, each week. Practice each behavior no more than ten or fifteen minutes, two to three times a day. Don't get discouraged—some behaviors take several weeks to perfect.

Back to the subject of manipulation—referring to your physical handling of your dog, not your dog's coercion over you. All dogs should accept handling just for ease in everyday life. Putting drops in eyes, cleaning ears, and trimming toenails should not be life-and-death struggles. Any good puppy care book instructs owners to play with their puppy's feet, ears, and mouth. If you have neglected this important detail of dog ownership until now, start immediately. Even if your dog is no longer a puppy, you can do this. Your relationship with your dog should be based on trust, and a dog that trusts you should accept handling, even if he doesn't like it. In fact, if you want to see some real natural acting ability, check out the heart-wrenching pathos of a reluctant dog having his nails clipped.

CHAPTER 3
STRUTTIN' YOUR STUFF

If you harbor a desire to have your dog become the next Lassie, Benji, or Rin Tin Tin, we've got to tell you it's not very likely. There just aren't that many recurring starring roles out there. But there are plenty of opportunities to strut your stuff, and some of them will make you money. Just not enough to retire on.

FAME . . .

If you have not tried the pet therapy work mentioned frequently throughout this book, you may want to look into it. You can bring joy to the residents of convalescent hospitals or a smile to a hospital's pediatric ward. It is a highly rewarding volunteer activity and you and your performing pooch can gain plenty of experience. Check with your local humane society to see if they have a program active in your area. If not, contact one of the national organizations promoting this activity (see end of chapter) or go it on your own. It's an excellent opportunity to hone your act.

If you are on your own, be aware that there are guidelines. Your dog must be clean and flea-free. He or she should be friendly but not boisterous. You must not inflict any scratches on patients, however unintentional they may be. You will need to get permission from someone at the facility before you begin your visits.

An alternative that is gaining in popularity is school visit programs. If you and your dog enjoy interacting with young people, consider combining entertainment with some education. You could have a major impact on the dog owners of the future by demonstrating the basics of training and acquainting them with a well-socialized dog: yours. Speak with the staff or teachers at your local school system if this idea interests you.

You can also check out talent competitions. That's right, talent competitions. At county or state fairs, pet walks, even some pet superstores, you can compete against other dog owners just as convinced that their dog is the most talented canine on the face of the planet. Prizes can range from dog bowls and leashes to cash and a year's supply of dog food. Judges are most likely to be impressed by an act rather than a few disjointed tricks. You can either chain behaviors to tell a story (like the war story illustrated in our final chapter), or work up a routine where you provide the flash and patter to connect your dog's talents together. It's even more impressive if you can work at some distance from your dog. But know your limits—mistakes will count against you unless you are mentally agile enough to cover them.

If you'd rather entertain than compete, you can hit the party circuit. Be the star attraction at your own gathering or offer to put on a show at your friends'.

The big attraction among the nonprofessional set is theater. High school, college, and local theater groups sometimes do need dogs for their productions. "Annie," "The Wizard of Oz," and "Peter Pan" are the best-known of the plays with major canine roles. If your dog has the look to suit the play, so much the better, but having a trained dog may prove more important than mere appearance.

To work in theater, you definitely need to be able to direct your dog from a distance. You will have to remain hidden in the wings while your canine thesbian takes his turn on the boards.

. . . AND FORTUNE

Before dollar signs start dancing before your eyes, you need to be aware of a little regulation. The United States Department of Agriculture (USDA) oversees any and all performing animals. To be paid for your services—even to appear in local theater without being paid—you must be licensed.

But there is another way. Contact any animal training agencies in your area. You can locate them in the Yellow Pages or by contacting your film commission or by reading film industry publications. In the Los Angeles area, the largest publication is the *LA411*. Contact them at 611 N. Larchmont Blvd. #201, Los Angeles, CA 90004, phone (213) 460-6304. *The Creative Handbook* North American edition covers the entire United States and Canada. You can reach them at 3518 Cahuenga Blvd. West #205, Los Angeles, CA 90004, phone (213) 874-4181. Both of these publications also list all of the film commissions in the United States.

Working under the auspices of an agency, you will be licensed under their USDA agreement and covered by their insurance (otherwise difficult to obtain).

Before you contact an animal training agency, you and your dog should be ready. Your dog must be well behaved with people, and it is very helpful if he is also socialized to other dogs and other animals such as cats and horses. He must have at least basic obedience training, and advanced obedience is preferred. Experience with acting behaviors is a definite plus.

When you approach an animal training agency, keep in mind that not all of them are receptive to the idea of working with outside dogs. Some companies may keep 50 or 75 of their own dogs and work only with them. But others may need a stable of outside talent to meet the demands of different jobs. If an agency is open to the idea of using outside talent, the first thing they will probably do is ask you to send pictures of your dog.

You do not have to go out and have professional studio shots made of your dog. Normal $3^1/2 \times 5$ or 4×6 photographs will be fine as long as they follow some basic guidelines. The photograph should show only your dog, in a sit and/or a stand position, with the dog filling most of the space. Try sending several of the same shot, plus a few shots of any special behaviors the dog does. If you have a pooch who excels at something like leaping high into the air to catch a Frisbee, a good action shot could be included. Enclose information along with the pictures. The agency will be interested in your dog's height, weight, age, and any training, as well as what other creatures your dog gets along with.

A company that likes your photos will probably then ask to see you and your dog. Bring some more photographs along, in case the agency decides to represent you. Some companies may offer dog training classes geared toward teaching behaviors that are used in the film and print industries. Others may suggest some training courses you should take.

If you do get a company interested, they may ask for an exclusive agreement. You will have to decide if this is acceptable. If it's the only agency in the county, you should probably just go ahead and sign. But if there is competition in your area, you may want to better your odds by being represented by as many companies as possible. See if this may be agreeable. Should you have the good fortune to be signed on by more than one agency, be sure to ask them to call you if the prospect of a job for your dog comes up. That way you can be sure that you won't have two companies sending out the same dog's picture for one job.

If you have gotten this far, you are very fortunate. If you actually land a job, you have bested all the odds. If fortune should smile on you, matters will now proceed as follows.

For a large job, there may be some pretraining involved, specific things that your dog will have to learn to fill the bill. This is ideal. You and the professional trainer can get to know each other, and more importantly, your dog can get to know the professional trainer.

You want your dog to be comfortable with the trainer because odds are that when it comes time to go on location, you won't be invited along. The trainer wants the dog's undivided attention, and your presence will probably be deemed distracting. If you have had the opportunity to watch the trainer work with your dog, and have become comfortable with the person yourself, this shouldn't be a problem. Many dogs perform better for the professional trainer, and the production company is paying for a professional to work the dog, after all.

If you are invited along (and it's up to the trainer to decide), take your cues from the trainer. There is a lot to know about being on a set. Stay out of the way. Do not, repeat, do not ask for autographs or take photographs. Never get in the way of any production people or talk while they are rolling sound. These people are professionals at their jobs and the best thing you can do is attempt to be invisible.

Should you be on the scene while your dog is being worked, it is important to remember that you got into this because it's fun. If you get stressed, you are going to pass that along to your dog. Relax, let the pros do their thing, and remember to have fun.

Most people think of performing opportunities only in movies and television, or maybe theater, but there are actually more opportunities in other areas. The print media is a huge market and includes greeting cards, calendars, t-shirts, puzzles, and print advertising. Advertising media itself covers print, in all its various forms, and television. Most businesses are well aware that animals in ads really attract attention. Corporate videos sometimes use animals, as do fashion shows.

If you just can't find an agency within a few hundred miles of where you live and you really want to get involved in performance work yourself, we can't say that your odds are good. But here are some suggestions to help you on your way.

Being able to train your dog is, of course, important. He will need to be well versed in obedience and in industry behaviors such as "Speak," "Head down," and "Wave." But knowing how best to handle the dog when you're actually on the scene is even more crucial. The animal's safety comes first (and never forget this in the excitement of the moment), but the next most important item is getting the shot. Work your dog in every possible location and situation so that you'll both be ready for anything.

You need to obtain an Exhibitors License from the United States Department of Agriculture. There are three regional offices (addresses and phone numbers are provided at the end of the chapter). The Western Region covers all the states west of a line drawn from North Dakota down to Texas. The Central Region covers the Dakotas, Nebraska, Iowa, Kansas, Missouri, Oklahoma, Arkansas, Texas, and Louisiana. The Eastern Region covers everything else, including Puerto Rico. You will be subject to annual inspections, and there will be regulations covering kennels, tags on your dogs, and a variety of other issues.

For anyone to know that you are in the business, you will need to get yourself listed with your local or state film commission and advertise in a film industry publication. The two mentioned previously (and again at the end of the chapter), the *LA411* and *The Creative Handbook,* are good choices, but their rates are fairly high.

You will have to obtain liability insurance. This may be your most difficult task, and even more expensive than the advertising.

You will need to have a service contract drawn up, and to familiarize yourself with how to set and quote daily rates, pretraining rates, and all sorts of other expenses.

Taking television, stage, or film courses will help you understand what to expect. It won't prepare you for the adrenalin rush of your first professional appearance on a set, but at least you'll have some experience.

There are some definite "rules of the road" if you are representing yourself on a set, and these apply whether the set is for a high-budget movie or a very low-budget photo shoot.

Be on time. In fact, be early if possible. It may give you a chance to rehearse on location without being in anyone's way. Then be prepared to wait.

Be prepared to do far more than you were told. The rule is that the job is never exactly as advertised. A job that on the phone was "the dog just has to sit and look at the actor" may become "have the dog come into the room, look around, lie down, sit back up, stare at the actor, bark, and run out of the room." You are expected to deliver whatever is requested.

Stay out of the way. Check in with your contact (usually the assistant director if you've reached the big time). Then don't ask questions of anyone, and don't answer them either. Discussing fees or how you just happened to fall into this job will not endear you to anyone. Be quiet and observe.

Keep your dog in your vehicle or in a crate out of the way. Otherwise you will constantly be telling people not to pet the dog. You're there to work, after all. You want to look like pros. And you want your dog's attention on you, not the grip who slipped him a corned beef sandwich from the catering truck.

Pack an equipment bag of any items you might need and carry it with you. Emblazon it with your business name. Be sure to include water for your dog.

Above all else, be safe and have fun. You almost certainly got into this because you enjoyed working with your dog. Don't lose sight of that fact.

USEFUL ADDRESSES

United States Department
  of Agriculture (USDA)
APHIS Animal Care
  Headquarters
4700 River Road, Unit 84
Riverdale, MD 20737-1234
301/734-4981 (phone)
301/734-4328 (fax)

Western Region
USDA/APHIS/Animal Care
9580 Micron Avenue,
  Suite J
Sacramento, CA 95827-2623
916/857-6205 (phone)
916/857-6212 (fax)

Central Region
USDA/APHIS/Animal Care
P.O. Box 6258
501 Felix Street, Bldg. #11
Fort Worth, TX 76115-6258
817/885-6923 (phone)
817/885-6917 (fax)

Eastern Region
USDA/APHIS/Animal Care
2568-A Riva Road, Suite 302
Annapolis, MD 21401-7400
410/571-8692 (phone)
410/962-0008 (fax)

LA411
611 N. Larchmont Blvd.
  #201
Los Angeles, CA 90004
213/460-6304

The Creative Handbook
North American Edition
3518 Cahuenga Blvd.
  West #205
Los Angeles, CA 90004
213/874-4181

Therapy Dogs International
6 Hilltop Road
Mendham, NJ 07945

Therapy Dogs, Inc.
P.O. Box 2786
Cheyenne, WY 82003

Delta Society
  (also doing pet therapy)
289 Perimeter Road
Renton, WA 98055-1329

Association of Pet Dog
  Trainers (APDT)
  (trainer referrals)
1-800-PET-DOGS
email: APDTBOD@aol.com

Puppyworks
(for dog training seminars)
www.puppyworks.com

CHAPTER 4
THE BASICS

If you and your dog have already learned basic obedience, feel free to skip this chapter. You should have "Sit," "Down," "Stand," and "Stay" well under control.

If you have not yet taught your dog basic obedience, it's never too late. Though we touch on teaching some obedience commands, attending a good class or taking lessons from a private trainer will accelerate your training. A good obedience foundation will allow you to get greater distance and better acting performance from your dog. It will also include the recall, or "Come," command, which we do not use here because it doesn't apply to any of the acting behaviors we will be covering.

Animal acting is a lot of fun, but basic obedience is absolutely essential. It may, in fact, save your dog's life some day. Obedience training is a necessity in our often hazardous world. Even if you never intend to compete in the formal obedience ring, you shouldn't neglect your dog's basic lessons.

Though it is called "obedience" and firm control is necessary, it can still be fun!

SIT

Prerequisites: None

Uses: Keeps the dog out from underfoot while you are preparing dinner, prevents him from bolting through doors, puts him in a handy position for cleaning ears or brushing teeth. (Yes, dogs' teeth should be brushed.) Serves as the basis for a wide variety of acting behaviors. The most basic of taught behaviors, capable of being learned by a six-week-old puppy.

Action: Stand or kneel (depending on your dog's size) in front of or beside your dog. Hold a treat right in front of your dog's nose, then move it slightly back over the dog's head. The dog should follow the treat, raising his nose and lowering his bottom to the ground. At first, reward as soon as you have the sit. Remember to associate the command ("Sit") with the action (dog sits) with the reward (give treat). As the sit becomes more reliable, stand up if you have been kneeling and wait a little while before giving the reward. You want to use the sit as the starting position for some of the acting behaviors, so you want the dog to stay in a sit until told otherwise.

If the dog doesn't respond to the food lure or continually gets up from the sit, then place the dog in position. With one hand pushing down on the pressure points at either side of the dog's back just ahead of the hipbones and the other pulling up on the leash, rock the dog back into a sit. Remember the same sequence applies: command ("Sit"), action (dog sits), reward (praise).

Timing: Be sure to give the treat while the dog's bottom is on the ground, not after he has gotten up.

Command: "Sit"

Signal: Hold your hand flat, palm up, and raise it from a position extended at your side to approximately level with your waist. Do not raise it so fast or so high that your dog doesn't see it.

Problems: If your dog tries to jump up after the treat, you are probably holding it too high over the dog's head. The motion is more straight back over the dog than up.

Some breeds, Doberman Pinschers for example, are known for never actually putting their butt on the ground when sitting, squatting on their haunches instead. This is an acceptable variation if it is normal for your dog.

1. With the dog in a standing position, give the command "Sit" and draw the treat back over the dog's nose until the dog sits. Reward.

OR

2. With one hand on the leash and one hand on the pressure point, rock the dog up and back into the Sit position.

3. Once the dog is in Sit position, remember to praise.

Molly the Bullmastiff demonstrates the Sit.

DOWN

Prerequisites: Sit

Uses:
Excellent for use as a control when you need to curb the boisterous eagerness of young dogs. The most comfortable position to use if you want the dog to stay in one place for more than a minute or so. Also serves as the basis for a variety of acting behaviors. Helps to reinforce your status as leader with dominant dogs.

Action:
Put the dog in a sit. Crouch or kneel in front of the dog. Hold the treat in front of the dog's nose and move it to the ground. Some dogs will lie down immediately. Quick, reward! Others will just lower their heads or slouch without quite lying down. Pull the treat slightly away from the dog to see if this will bring the dog down. If your dog is easily frustrated, reward some of her less-than-complete downs to keep her interested.

If the dog doesn't respond to the food lure or continually gets up from the down, place the dog in position. With one thumb on the pressure point between the dog's shoulder blades, push down and to one side or the other while pulling down on the leash with your other hand. Or use the pressure points at either side of the dog's back just behind the shoulder blades.

Timing:
While the dog is learning, you can reward intermediate positions between the Sit and the Down—slouching but not actually lying down, for example. But demand a more and more correct position until you are only rewarding a full down.

Command:
"Down" is commonly used, but many people use this word unthinkingly when they want the dog off something rather than lying down. Popular alternatives are "Crash," "Drop," "Lie" (as in "lie down"), or the German "Platz."

Signal:
With your palm flat and facing the dog, swing your arm downward from chest level to waist level.

Problems:
Dogs are often resistant to this behavior. If you have clearly established yourself as pack leader, it should not be an issue. If you do have problems, definitely reward some early approximations of the behavior, such as the dog dipping her head or moving one leg forward. If the dog moves forward rather than lies down, change how you are moving the treat to the ground—you are probably drawing it away from the dog too much.

1. With the dog in a Sit, hold the treat in front of the dog's nose and move it to the ground, giving the command "Down."

2. Quickly reward when the dog is in the down position.

OR

3. While pulling down on the leash, gently use the pressure point to place the dog into the down position.

4. Quickly give the command and praise the dog when she's in the down position.

Molly the Bullmastiff demonstrates the Down.

STAND

Prerequisites: Sit is helpful.

Uses: A really helpful command when grooming or examining your dog. An essential talent for any dog being shown in the conformation ring, where the dog must not only stand, but stand with each foot in correct position. Your veterinarian will also appreciate a dog that stands for a check-up.

Action: With the dog in a sit, place yourself facing the dog's shoulder or ear. Hold a treat in front of the dog's nose and move it forward, directly away from the dog. If the dog follows the treat, he will automatically rise out of the sit. Give the treat when he stands up.

If the dog doesn't follow the treat, have a leash to give a gentle tug forward and use your foot to gently nudge the dog in the belly just in front of the hind legs as you offer the treat. This will provide an added incentive to stand.

Once you are getting a reliable performance, move to other positions around the dog, particularly standing in front of him.

Timing: Be sure to give the treat while the dog is standing, preferably without a lot of fidgeting.

Command: "Stand." In the conformation ring this may be "Stack," meaning a stand in a particular pose.

Signal: Draw your hand back away from the dog. If you used your foot in training, use it as part of your signal.

Problems: If the dog jumps up rather than just stands, you are holding the treat too high.

Many dogs move toward you once they're standing. Work on your stay or use "Back up" (in Chapter 8) to reposition the dog.

1. With the dog in the sit position, lure the dog forward with the treat and give the command "Stand."

2. When the dog is in the standing position, quickly reward her.

3. With the treat and leash in the same hand, gently pull forward and touch the dog's belly with your foot, give the command "Stand," and praise.

Molly the Bullmastiff demonstrating the Stand.

STAY

Prerequisites: Any of the position commands—"Sit," "Down," "Stand"

Uses: Excellent for keeping the dog out of the way for brief periods, such as while you answer the door, stir the spaghetti sauce, or whatever. Necessary for gaining distance with commands—that is, put the dog in a sit, tell her to stay, and move a number of feet away before asking her to wave or speak. Mandatory in obedience competitions.

Action: Put the dog in the position you wish to use. (Down is the most comfortable position for the dog and hardest to move from, thus easiest for the stay. Stand is the trickiest.) Give your command and signal, move slightly away, return and reward and release. Gradually move farther away and wait longer before returning.

Remember to let the dog relax between stays, and to use different positions.

Vital Information: A dog must be released from a stay. The command means the dog is not to leave the position until given further commands or released. Never put your dog in a stay and walk away and forget about her.

Timing: Do not show the dog the treat until you are ready to release her from the position. It may induce her to move. Give the treat while the dog is still in the desired position, but as you are about to release her.

Command: "Stay." (For release, "Take a break," "Free," or "Release" are often used.)

Signal: If you are near the dog, sweep your open hand directly toward the dog, stopping just short of touching her nose with your palm. At a distance, hold your hand up palm outward, like a traffic cop ordering someone to stop.

Problems: The dog breaks the Stay. You're moving too fast and asking too much. If your hyperactive pooch can only hold still for two seconds, then only ask for two seconds and work for quite a while before extending it to three. If the dog continues to break the stay, use the pressure points to place the dog back in position each time he gets up. "Stay" is combined with any of the positions to mean the dog will remain in one place in the chosen position until given a further command or released: "Sit Stay," "Down Stay," or "Stand Stay."

Ranger the Bernese Mountain Dog demonstrating a sit stay.

CHAPTER 5
JUST SITTIN' AROUND

Working with the dog in a sit position gives you control. You can place yourself in the best spot for interacting with your dog and not have to worry about a lot of moving around. The dog feels relatively secure and can concentrate on the work you're trying to do.

Dogs that have practiced a variety of behaviors from the sit position are more likely to keep their focus on you to see if you are going to ask them to do something besides just sit there. This can certainly work to your advantage in the obedience ring. But beware—dogs can also become quite the innovators, throwing behaviors at you to see if they might get rewarded. And the reaction of the spectators—who nearly always laugh if a dog on a long Sit suddenly starts waving or sits up and begs—may be all the reward your dog needs to encourage a repeat of his performance.

Therapy dogs win over patients and staff just by the simple act of kissing patients or waving goodbye.

Conformation dogs don't sit when in the show ring, of course. But the muscle tone in their lower backs and thighs will be improved by sitting up. And doing a little showing off while the judge is busy with other dogs (without disrupting the class) can get the crowd on your side.

For actual acting work, Wave, Sit up, Play dead, and Where's your nose? are requested behaviors. And they have excellent potential for storytelling. (See Chapter 11 for suggestions.)

WAVE/HIGH FIVE

Prerequisites: Sit, Stay

Uses: A good "story" behavior, useful for weaving into a sequence of events. Can cheer the home team with a high five or wave at departing guests. A really strong wave or high five can improve reach in the front legs. Alternating left and right legs in quick succession gives some quick aerobic exercise.

Action: Kneel or stand in front of your dog (depending on the dog's height). Put the dog in a sit. Hold a treat in your closed hand. Hold the treat near the dog's mouth and encourage the dog to get the treat (while staying in a sit). Remember the sequence is command, action, reward, so encourage the dog with "Get it" but also command "Wave." You will be saying something like, "Get it, wave, get it, wave." Once the dog knows the behavior, you will simply command "Wave."

When a front paw comes off the ground, reward the dog with the treat. As you practice, try to reward a little better performance each time. Some dogs will try a lot of nuzzling, barking, and just sitting and staring. Be patient.

Once you are getting a reliable performance, stand up. For wave, toss the treat as you gradually increase your distance from the dog. For high five, bend over only enough for the dog to be able to reach your outstretched hand with his paw.

Timing: Be sure to give the treat while the dog's paw is in the air or pawing at your hand. When your dog understands the command, withholding the treat will get the dog to repeat the action, thus creating an active wave.

Command: "Wave" or "High five"

Signal: For "Wave," hold your hand flat and wave it at the dog. For "High five," flatten your hand and extend it toward the dog. Your dog should perform these behaviors with either of his front feet. A signal with your right hand means the dog uses his left paw. Left hand means right paw. Lean your own body to encourage the dog to shift his weight onto the foot that will not be raised.

Problems: If the dog gets up, place him back in a Sit. Some dogs don't use their paws very much and will not paw at your hand. With these dogs, you can use manipulation, picking the paw up as you give your command. When they are used to this action, they will reach toward your hand, and you can pull your hand back to get them to extend their leg. This method will take longer and won't result in a high flashy wave. You might want to call it "Shake."

1. With the dog in the sit position, hide a treat in your hand. Hold it down low.

2. Encourage the dog to "Get it" and give the command "Wave." Reward the dog when his foot comes off the ground.

3. When the dog starts touching your hand with his paw, stand up and start moving farther away each time.

4. Once the dog is doing well, stand far enough away so the dog can't touch you. Give the signal, command, and toss the treat to the dog.

Boone the yellow Labrador Retriever demonstrating a Wave.

SIT UP/BEG

Prerequisites: Sit, Stay

Uses:
A "cute" behavior, good for eliciting giggles and "ahs" from viewers. Also excellent for improving balance and strengthening the muscles in the thighs and on either side of the lower back. A dog that wobbles when attempting this probably lacks good muscle tone in these areas. Other behaviors, such as waving or balancing a biscuit on the bridge of the nose, can be combined with sit up to good effect.

Action:
Kneel or stand in front of your dog (depending on dog's height). Put the dog in a Sit. Now pinch a treat between your fingers so it is hard for the dog to get it. Hold it right in front of the dog's nose and then move your hand upward slightly. When the dog's front feet come off the ground, give the treat while saying "Sit up." As you practice, try to reward a little better performance each time.

When the dog sits all the way up, say "Stay" and have him balance there a moment before giving the treat. Once you are getting a reliable performance, stand up if you have been kneeling and gradually increase your distance from the dog. Toss the treat to the dog. Your aim must be excellent to avoid knocking the dog off balance.

Timing:
Be sure to give the treat when the dog's front feet are off the ground, not when they have come back down. If you only reward once the dog's feet are back on the ground, he will think that the action you are after is to rear up and then come down.

Command:
"Sit up"; "Beg"; "Sit pretty"

Signal:
Hold both hands partially closed (as if they might be holding a treat) and move them out from your body to an extended arm position, toward the dog.

Problems:
If the dog rises up off his haunches, you are holding the treat too high. Keep it right on the dog's nose.

If the dog has trouble holding the position, practice with him sitting in the corner to help his balance and control. Don't get discouraged—this behavior is a real crowd-pleaser.

1. Pinching the treat between your fingers, draw it directly over the dog's nose.

2. When the dog's feet come off the ground, give the treat while saying the command "Sit up."

3. Using hand signals, give the command "Sit up, Stay." Then toss the treat to the dog while she is sitting up.

Misty the Beagle demonstrates Sit up.

BANG/PLAY DEAD

Prerequisites: Sit, Down, On Your Side, Head Down

Uses: People love to "shoot" their dogs. Also good as part of a storytelling chain of behaviors. Especially impressive with the dog facing away from the shooter. A nice variation on "puppy push-ups"—instead of alternating "Sit" and "Down," use "Sit" and "Bang."

Action: Put the dog in a Sit and stand close in front of her. Say "Bang down" and give your signal for "Down." When the dog is down, say "Bang on your side" and give your signal for this. If the dog keeps her head up to look at you, say "Bang head down." When the dog is flat out on her side, tell her to stay. Give the treat as you give her your release word.

After you have practiced and your dog seems to be getting it, phase out all the extra commands and just use body language to help her. Practice at odd moments, not just when you are working a full session with your dog.

Timing: Try to offer the treat while the dog is still on her side. Many dogs will straighten up to eat, however.

Command: "Bang"

Signal: Form your hand into a gun, point it at the dog, and shoot.

Problems: "Dead" dogs often have wagging tails. Try frowning at the dog to see if that will stop it. Or leave it alone, knowing that people will laugh at the liveliness of your "dead" dog.

If your dog is not responding, you will need to work on "On your side" (p.36) more, and help the dog by placing her in position. If she responds slowly, make a bigger deal about her getting into position and be faster with the reward.

If, in front of an audience, you give the command and the dog doesn't respond, cover up by saying, "Drat! Missed!" and shoot her again. If the dog goes down but doesn't die all the way, say, "Only winged her" and shoot again.

1. With the dog in a Sit, point your finger gun at the dog, give the command "Bang down" and give your signal for Down.

2. When the dog is down, say "Bang on your side" and give your signal for On your side.

3. Practice taking out the extra commands, just using the word "Bang" and your body language.

Molly the Bullmastiff demonstrating Play dead.

WHERE'S YOUR NOSE?

Prerequisites: Sit, Stay; High Five/Wave is helpful

Uses: Good for storytelling performances, such as asking the dog to be sure his nose is ready before having him search for something. Also the basis for a more advanced trick, "Hide your eyes," in which the dog lies down and covers his eyes with both paws.

Action: You will need a prop to help you—a clothespin, bobbie pin, paper clip, or cloth tape. One in particular may work better with your dog. Put the prop on the dog's muzzle clipped to some hair or the whiskers at the side of the muzzle (on your dog's dominant side—is your dog left- or right-pawed?). When the dog paws at his nose, give the command "Where's your nose?," take off the prop you are using, and give a treat.

Timing: There is a lot for you to do here. The quicker you can remove whatever device you are using and offer a treat, the stronger the association the dog will make with swiping his paw over his nose. Some dogs are capable of staying in that position. Give the command "stay" while the dog's paw is on his nose for a more impressive performance.

Command: "Where's your nose?" if the dog can stay, or "Wipe your face" if the dog just paws at his nose

Signal: Wipe your own flattened hand down your own nose.

Problems: Some dogs are very stoic and will simply sit there with the prop on their nose. Try different items to see if another gets more response. Ponytail scrunchies often work well because they are large and block the dog's vision. If you have not already taught the High five/Wave, go back and do that—it may give your dog the idea to use his paw. You can also try blowing on the prop or in the dog's ear, but be careful—some dogs tend to snap when you do this. Touching the object with your finger can also make the dog more aware of the prop.

1. With the dog in a Sit, place your prop on the dog's muzzle.

2. Encourage the dog to wipe the prop and give your command and signal.

3. When the dog wipes the prop, reward the dog and remove the prop.

4. Once you're no longer using the prop, ask for a better performance each time and try to get the dog to stay in the position.

Jessie the mixed breed demonstrating Where's your nose?

CHAPTER 6
DOWN IN FRONT

While "Down" is usually the most difficult position to teach, once it is learned it is pretty secure. A dog in a down will tend to stay in a down. So it is a good position for working on further behaviors. Dogs seem to find the "tricks" in this chapter pretty easy stuff. If you want some quick success, try these.

Though these behaviors may be relatively easy to teach, they can be quite impressive. If you want your dog to look ashamed or depressed on cue, practice "Head down." Then you could have him crawl to you for forgiveness. "Roll over" is always a big favorite at pet therapy sessions, and can even be helpful in grooming if you allow your dog to lie down while being brushed. "On your side" is rarely used on its own, but is the foundation for other behaviors such as "Bang, you're dead" and "Roll over."

Crawling is excellent indoor exercise for dogs. It works on shoulders, spine, neck, and hindquarters. (You should, of course, be sure your dog has no physical problems in these areas before you ask him to perform.) Be very sure that your dog understands he will only be rewarded for these behaviors when you ask for them. Otherwise you may find yourself in the group long down in the obedience ring with the only dog crawling across the ring to join you.

In this chapter we will use physical manipulation for the first time. If you had problems with "Down," you may encounter some resistance here. Dominant dogs do not simply accept being pushed into position. But patience and enticing treats should get you through. If you have *real* problems—if the dog growls when you try to guide him into position—you need to work on more important matters than tricks. But as long as you have a solid relationship with your dog, it will be to both of your advantages for him to learn to accept handling.

HEAD DOWN/HEAD UP

Prerequisites: Down

Uses: This is an acting behavior. A dog with his chin on the floor, eyes rolled up to watch you, can't help but look sad or ashamed. You provide the appropriate commentary, such as, "I caught you stealing that cookie from the cookie jar. Now what do you do? That's right, look ashamed." If you use this behavior to its best advantage, you can get some great "ahs."

Action: Put the dog in a Down. Crouch or kneel beside him. With one hand, hold your treat on the floor a couple of feet in front of the dog. With the other hand across the dog's neck directly behind the ears, gently push the dog's head down so that his chin is on the floor between his front paws. Give your command, hold his head there for a second or two, then give a treat and praise as you let go. If your dog resists your manipulation, you can use the treat as a lure but still use your free hand on the dog's head to be sure that chin is on the floor. When your dog seems to understand your request, use your "Stay" command and remove your hands. Have the dog hold the "Head down" for a couple of seconds before giving the treat and releasing.

For "Head up," do a "Head down" and hold the treat in front of the dog's nose, but then move the treat up. Always do more "Head down" than "Head up," and give the treat at different times. That way, the dog will offer both behaviors equally well, not knowing when the treat will be offered.

Timing: Give the treat while the dog's chin is on the ground, then release quickly because the dog will usually pick his head up to chew.

Command: "Head down"; "Head up"

Signal: Be sure your signals here are obviously different from your down and sit signals. Point to the floor for "Head down." Keep your hand in the same shape and move it up, index finger pointing toward the dog, for "Head up."

Problems: Some dogs have a habit of turning their head to one side or the other so it rests on a paw rather than the floor. While you are in the learning phase of this behavior, position the dog so his chin is on the floor between his paws. It is visually more effective, and if you want to later teach "Hide your eyes," you need the dog's paws free. For a dog that resists this behavior, it's important that he is rewarded the second his chin touches the floor. Don't hold him there if he is struggling. Place him in position, give the command, have his head touch the floor, and reward. He will eventually stop fighting as he gets used to this. Then start telling him to stay for a gradually longer performance of the behavior.

1. With the dog in a Down, place one hand on the pressure point behind the head and with the other hand hold the treat on the floor.

2. Push gently down on the dog's head while giving the command "Head down." Try to hold him there for a few seconds before giving the treat.

3. Once the dog is doing well, stop placing the dog into position. Just give the signal and the command and toss the treat to the dog.

Toby the Basset Hound demonstrating Head down.

ON YOUR SIDE/STRAIGHTEN UP/OTHER SIDE

Prerequisites: Down

Uses: This behavior serves mainly as the basis for other behaviors. Both "Roll over" and "Bang, you're dead" require "On your side" as a foundation. It's also useful in making large dogs seem less intimidating in pet therapy work. A dog lying flat out and showing his tummy is pretty nonthreatening, especially if his tail is thumping at the same time. It can also be part of doggy aerobics—alternate "Sit," "Down," "On your side," "Straighten up," "Other side," "Sit."

Action: Put your dog in a down and kneel down to one side. Look at the dog's hips. If they are shifted to one side, you will roll him toward the leg that's tucked under him. Take the front leg on the same side as the hip that's tucked in one hand and place your hand on the dog's neck and push him gently onto his side while saying, "On your side." Give a treat when he's flat on the floor.

     Shift your weight back to the center and encourage the dog to come back to a normal down position while saying "Straighten up." Repeat the behavior going in the other direction.

Timing: Give your treat while the dog is flat on his side and give your release word.

Command: "On your side"; "Straighten up"; "Other side"

Signal: Flatten both hands and extend them away from your body and flop them in the same motion you used to place the dog in the position. Shifting your body helps cue the dog in the direction you want him to go. For "Straighten up," bring your hands back to the starting position.

Problems: All animals favor one side over the other. Figure out your dog's better side and use that for the initial learning period. Probably the most difficult part of this behavior is getting the dog to shift his hips to go in the other direction. This posture is a submissive position, so dominant dogs may be reluctant to cooperate. Insist gently: you're in charge.

     If you find yourself wrestling with your dog, and your dog is winning, stop. Try using the method used to teach "Roll over" (this chapter), but only lure him halfway.

1. With the dog in a Down, place one hand on her neck and hold the dog's outside leg. Notice that the trainer is rolling the dog toward the tucked-under hip.

2. Gently push the dog onto its side while giving the command "On your side." Reward the dog.

3. Now shift your weight back to the center and encourage the dog to come up to the normal down position while saying "Straighten up." Reward.

4. Once your dog is doing well, no longer place your dog into position. Give the signal and the command and reward your dog.

Misty the Golden Retriever demonstrating On your side.

CRAWL

Prerequisites: Down

Uses: Actually required for the "crawl tunnel" obstacle in one form of agility. Useful for search and rescue work. Regularly seen in commercial and TV or movie acting work. Surprisingly effective at building up shoulders, hindquarters, and the spinal column. Excellent for combining behaviors for storytelling, especially if you lean toward war stories or Westerns.

Action: Put the dog in a Down. Crouch or kneel slightly in front of and to the side of the dog. Hold a treat in whichever hand is more in front of the dog, with the other hand slightly above the dog's shoulders. Entice the dog forward to get the treat. If the dog starts to get up, use your other hand to exert enough pressure to keep the dog down. Don't hold it on the dog, just push and release.

Alternately, you can use your own leg as a tunnel. Put the dog in a Down. Sit in front of him and bend the leg nearer the dog to form an arch. Hold the treat on the side of that leg away from the dog and entice her to crawl through. If you have a large dog, you can use a coffee table as the tunnel.

Timing: Be sure the dog is in a Down when you give the treat.

Command: "Crawl"

Signal: Hang both your hands down toward the floor and wiggle your fingers enticingly.

Problems: Some dogs, presumably those with weak shoulders, will keep their front end on the ground but lift their rears up and move in an odd sort of crouch. Use an obstacle low enough to force the dog to keep both ends on the ground and ask for only very short distances at first. Also keep the dog moving *slowly*, as this helps to keep the dog down.

1. With the dog in a Down, hold a treat in front of the dog and hold your other hand slightly above the dog's shoulder. Entice the dog forward to get the treat. Give the command "Crawl."

2. If the dog starts to get up, push on the dog's shoulders to keep him down and then release. Don't hold your hand on the dog's shoulders.

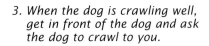

3. When the dog is crawling well, get in front of the dog and ask the dog to crawl to you.

Doogie the Australian Shepherd demonstrating Crawl.

ROLL OVER

Prerequisites: Down, On Your Side

Uses: This behavior seems to delight children for some reason, especially if you can have your dog do two or three in a row.

Action: Put the dog in a down and do "On your side" to whichever side your dog favors. Now take a treat, show it to your dog, and move the treat over the dog's shoulder toward her backbone. The dog should twist her neck to follow the treat. If the neck twists far enough, the body will follow. Once the body starts over, you should have the dog's feet in the air. (This position, with the dog on her back, feet in the air, belly totally exposed, is called "Centerfold," and you may choose to train this as a separate behavior.) Move quickly to the side the dog is rolling toward so you can continue to lure her all the way over with the treat. Take one of the front legs and nudge it in the direction the dog is going to complete the roll over if she doesn't do it on her own.

Timing: Remember to give the command as the dog is rolling over and the treat when she straightens up. Do not let her up from the down. If you want to do more than one Roll over at a time once you are experienced, the dog will need to remain down.

Command: "Roll over"

Signal: Draw a circle in the air in front of you, going in whichever direction you are asking the dog to go.

Problems: If your dog doesn't follow the treat well enough to get her feet in the air, use a more enticing treat. If the dog goes halfway but then stops, try physically moving the dog the rest of the way. If your dog is ordinarily strongly food motivated but resists this behavior, suspect some physical problem and discuss it with your veterinarian.

If your dog is fine physically but reluctant to roll over, realize this is a very vulnerable position. You can gradually shape the behavior by giving a treat for any movement at first, then asking for a response closer to the behavior each time.

1. With the dog in a down, give the command "On your side" and lure the dog's head with the treat over her shoulder toward her backbone.

2. Continue to lure the dog back so that her body follows her head and give the command "Roll over."

3. Continue all the way over until the dog is back in a down position and reward her.

Sunday the mixed breed during Roll over.

4. Once the dog will roll over,
stand up and cue the dog.

*Sunday the mixed breed
demonstrating Roll over.*

CHAPTER 7
THE STAND-IN

Working from the Stand is less secure than working from other positions. It's just so easy for the dog to move or to go into a Sit or a Down. It's best to practice behaviors from other positions first so that you are more experienced in your actions and timing. Be sure your dog's Stand is solid. Then you're ready.

The following behaviors have a wide variety of uses. Feet up, for example, can prove helpful in everyday life. An aging 80-pound dog is more than a handful to lift up onto something, but if he puts his front feet up on the car or grooming table, it's easy to boost the rear end up.

Walk seems to delight young and old spectators alike, and is wonderful for pet therapy work. Circle can be good indoor exercise, especially if your dog whips herself into a frenzy when doing multiple circles. And what better way to end a performance than by taking a Bow? Dogs already know how to do this—you've probably seen your dog doing a play bow during play time—you're just attaching a command to it.

Most of these behaviors are more effective if there is some distance between you and your dog. For any behavior, practice until your dog is performing it reliably, then gradually edge away from the dog. If problems crop up, stay close until you've worked them out, then start increasing distance again. Anyone doing professional animal acting work is nearly always a considerable distance from their performers. Even those of us just doing it for fun find it much more impressive when handler and dog are separated.

FEET UP

Prerequisites: Stand, Stay

Uses: As mentioned, a variety of practical uses, particularly for large dogs. Getting up on a grooming table, exam table, or the back of a pickup are all easier with Feet up. Also wonderful for pet therapy work. Dogs can put their feet up on beds or wheelchair arms, making it easier for their admirers to reach them.

Action: Put the dog in a Stand facing some surface at a convenient height. Be sure the surface, whatever it is, will not tip under the dog's weight. Large footstools, dining room chairs, and flat-topped trunks work well. Hold a treat in front of the dog and move it forward above the surface you have chosen. Pat the surface. Encourage the dog to get the treat. Once you are getting the dog's feet on the surface, delay the treat for a few seconds while telling the dog to stay.

Timing: Give the treat while the dog's feet are solidly on the surface.

Command: "Feet up"

Signal: With both hands, point from the dog to the surface on which you want Feet up performed.

Problems: Some dogs interpret your patting of a surface as an invitation to jump completely onto it. Try just moving the treat slightly over the surface without any further encouragement. If the dog still jumps up, use your leash to guide him into the correct position, then praise and give the treat.

Other dogs are extremely reluctant to put their feet up on furniture, especially if you have been firm in teaching the dog not to get on couches or chairs. Try lifting the dog's paws onto the surface the first couple of times you attempt the behavior. Also try practicing this behavior outside on picnic benches, tree stumps, or whatever is the right height for your dog.

1. With the dog in a Stand, show her the surface you want her to put her feet up on.

2. Hold a treat in front of the dog and lure her forward so that she puts her front feet on the chair, while giving the command "Feet up."

3. Once she's doing well, have her stay in that position and toss the treat to her.

Shady the Siberian Husky demonstrating Feet up.

PUT 'EM UP/WALK

Prerequisites: Stand, Stay

Uses: This rise out of the Stand position requires strength in the entire hindquarters. Standing in one place (Put 'em up) also calls for excellent balance. This is good foundation training for a dog that will be competing in agility. But a cute little dog walking on its hind legs is always going to steal the show.

Action: Put the dog in a Stand and, with a treat in one hand, draw your hands up over the dog and raise them straight up above the dog, enticing her to straighten her back legs and stand up. Reward and release. When she is doing well, hold the treat so the dog has to work at getting it from your hand while she is standing up, which will keep her in the position longer and teach her to balance. Now give the command "Put 'em up, stay" and move away from the dog, rewarding by tossing the treat while she is standing up. This stationary standing up is Put 'em up.

Now that you have Put 'em up on command, you can teach the dog to walk on her hind legs by asking her to come forward while she's still in the Put 'em up position. Ask for just one or two steps in the beginning, then toss the treat.

Timing: Be sure to give the treat while the dog is on her hind legs, not after she has come back to a Sit or a normal Stand. When you are working on gaining distance, tossing a treat to your standing dog will be quite a test of your accuracy.

Command: "Put 'em up"; "High"; "Walk"

Signal: Hold your arm straight out as if you're pointing up high to something.

Problems: Dogs with back or hip problems should not be asked to perform this behavior. If your dog has a difficult time balancing, use your most enticing treat and make it hard for the dog to get it. They will concentrate more on the treat and less on the fact that they're standing up. Don't reward the dog if he's jumping to get the treat.

1. With the dog in a Stand, hold the treat well above the dog's head.

2. When the dog comes up, give the command "Put 'em up" and try to keep the dog standing up for several seconds. Give the reward.

3. When the dog is doing well, move away from the dog, command the dog to "Put 'em up, stay," and toss the treat to the dog.

Sunday the mixed breed demonstrating Put 'em up.

TAKE A BOW

Prerequisites: Stand

Uses: The perfect behavior to finish any performance. It also stretches the muscles all along the spine.

Action: Put the dog in a Stand, put a treat in your hands, and quickly push the treat toward the dog between her front legs until her front end starts going down. Say "Bow" and give her the treat. The next step is to make sure her front legs are completely on the ground before rewarding her.

Or, if you are not in a hurry, you can experience how it feels to teach by mimicking behavior. The play Bow is such a natural behavior that it is one of the easiest to teach in this way.

When your dog is in a playful mood, assume the play Bow position yourself. Waggle your rear end. See if your dog will return the bow. Reward any move she makes toward giving you a Bow. Teaching by mimicking generally takes longer than teaching by lure and/or manipulation, but there are some behaviors, such as yawn, that can only be taught this way.

Timing: Give the treat while the dog's front end is on the ground, but be sure that the back end doesn't collapse. Release the dog before she goes down.

Command: "Take a bow" or just "Bow"

Signal: Make both hands into fists and move them down while flicking your wrists so that your hands move up.

Problems: You can use a leash looped around the dog's belly to hold up the back end if the dog keeps Downing. If someone else is usually available while you are training, you can have the second person stay at the dog's side and place a hand under the dog's belly just forward of the hips in place of the leash.

1. With the dog in a Stand, quickly push the treat toward the dog between her front legs while giving the command "Bow."

2. When the dog's front legs go flat on the floor and her back end is up, reward her.

3. Once the dog is doing well, give the signal and the command and toss the treat to the dog.

Magic the mixed breed demonstrating Bow.

CIRCLE LEFT/CIRCLE RIGHT

Prerequisites: Stand

Uses: This is a good exercise for developing suppleness in your dog, and can prove helpful for agility dogs. If you plan on teaching the more advanced Figure eight through the legs or Grapevine, some preliminary practice with circling will make it easier. There is a new sport called Canine Freestyle, in which handler and dog perform a routine of their own devising to music. Circling could be very effective as part of such a routine.

Action: Put the dog in a Stand in front of you. Put a treat in your left hand and lead the dog in a circle clockwise by moving the treat around. If this works, practice this way, using the left hand for circling clockwise and the right hand for circling counterclockwise.

   If your dog does not follow the treat, put the dog's leash in the same hand as the treat and physically lead the dog around while moving the treat in the circle. After you have done this for a while, try again with just the treat.

Timing: Give the treat when the dog has finished the circle. Right from the beginning, vary the number of circles you ask the dog to do before rewarding it. That way the dog tends to perform better, not knowing when he's going to be rewarded.

Command: "Circle left"; "Circle right"

Signal: With your index finger pointing, draw a circle in the direction you want your dog to go. Make it more dramatic by shifting your body weight in the same direction you're pointing.

Problems: Be sure to show your dog from the beginning that more than one circle may be required to earn a treat, whether it's two or three in the same direction or a circle left followed by a circle right. Otherwise you may have a lot of trouble getting multiple circles later. If the dog's not circling, you may be holding the treat too high, moving too fast, or not making the circle large enough.

1. With the dog in a Stand, lure the dog around in a circle.

2. Continue to lure the dog while giving the command "Circle left" or "Circle right."

3. Reward the dog once she has completed the circle.

Sheppie the mixed breed during Circle.

4. *Once your dog is doing well, stop luring her. Give the signal and command and toss the treat.*

Sheppie the mixed breed demonstrating Circle.

CHAPTER 8
A MOVING EXPERIENCE

Now that you have some experience working on behaviors that are stationary or nearly so, it's time to try some that really move. Your control over the dog is a little looser when you start introducing movement, so you will need to be on your toes.

Backing up is something your dog does naturally. But it can be rather difficult to put on cue. Show patience and you will be rewarded. Back up can be useful in a surprising number of circumstances. If you're hoping to pursue some real animal acting, Back up is one of the essential behaviors.

Your success with Figure eight through the legs and the more advanced Grapevine will depend partially on your dog's height and the length of your legs. Great Danes and Irish Wolfhounds are not leading candidates for these behaviors. But most toy or terrier breeds are. And if you are a long-legged six-footer, there shouldn't be any problem with any of the mid-size retrievers, hounds, or others.

The clicker is traditionally used in theater work, but has now become popular in basic training. If you used a clicker in teaching your dog to sit, lie down, and so on, don't use it now. But don't despair—you just need to choose some other small noisemaker that doesn't have any learned associations for your dog.

You will need a good supply of patience and food treats as well as a few props for this chapter. Master these behaviors and you will have shown some real training prowess.

BACK UP

Prerequisites: Stand

Uses: In obedience, being able to move the dog backward can come in handy in practicing a variety of exercises—obviously in heeling and finish work and certainly in those pesky Utility go-outs. In conformation, you may find that your dog stacks himself better if he backs into the pose. Backing up is good exercise and helps the dog learn where his hindquarters are (surprisingly, many dogs have little idea of exactly where they are placing their rear feet).

Action: Make a squeeze chute. You can use a coffee table and the front of a couch, an exercise pen along a wall, or whatever you have available. Just be sure the improvised chute will not topple over on the dog if bumped and that it is high enough to keep the dog from jumping out and narrow enough to keep the dog from turning around.

Position the dog at one end of the squeeze chute, facing out. Stand in front of him. Move into the dog, bumping him gently with your knee or foot (depending on the dog's size). If the dog moves back, praise and give a treat while saying "Back up." If the dog sits, a common reaction, bump him again so that he hops backward or ask him to stand. Now praise and reward.

Some dogs will try to turn around in the squeeze chute, others will try to jump out. With these dogs, use a leash to keep them in place and facing front, move slowly, and praise at the slightest sign of cooperation. They require some confidence building.

When your dog seems to be catching on, stop short of bumping him. See if you can shoo him back with the same leg movement but without contact.

Timing: At first, ask for only minor movements and offer plenty of encouragement and lots of rewards. Have treats ready at all times. It's very important in this behavior to toss the treat to the dog, encouraging him to back up to get it. You will get a much stronger performance.

Command: "Back up"; "Get back"

Signal: A shooing motion with your hands and the leg motion you made when bumping the dog.

Problems: Insecure dogs often have a difficult time with this behavior and try frantically just to get out of your way when or even before you bump them. Go very slowly and do everything you can to build up confidence. You can work on this without the squeeze pen, but it will be harder to ensure that the dog backs straight.

1. With the dog standing in some type of squeeze chute, move into the dog, bumping him gently with your knee while giving the command "Back up." Reward him only when he's backing up.

2. Once the dog is doing well, back him up without the squeeze chute.

3. Give your signal using your hands and your knee as your cue, as if you're moving forward (but don't), and when the dog backs away from you, toss the treat to him.

Ranger the Bernese Mountain Dog demonstrating Back up.

FIGURE EIGHT THROUGH THE LEGS

Prerequisites: Stand

Uses:
This serves as the foundation for the next behavior, the Grapevine. But on its own it can help boost your dog's confidence and increase flexibility. Bending is often advised to help dogs gain good jumping form, especially in agility, where dogs often have to turn sharply between jumps. Trying to perform a figure eight around your legs forces a dog to bend extensively. Be sure to practice in both directions, with the dog starting in front of you and behind you.

Action:
Stand with your legs spread a little more than shoulder width. Have the dog sit or stand behind you. Hold a treat in each hand and offer the treat with your right hand from the front between your legs while hiding the treat in your left hand behind your back. Lure your dog through your legs and around to the back of your right leg. Meet your left hand to your right hand through your legs, then hide your right hand and continue to lure the dog with your left hand to the back of your left leg. Now meet your right hand to the left, hide your left hand, and continue to lure the dog through your legs. Reward—you've completed the figure eight.

Once the dog shows some understanding, try to make the entire figure eight in one movement. This requires agility on your part to switch from leading with your right hand to leading with your left. You can also try using one treat, switching it from hand to hand at the changeover point.

Once the dog is doing well, don't stop at one complete figure eight—go for two, three, even four if your dog can take it. You don't want a dog that stops automatically after one pass.

Timing:
If your dog is hesitant, reward at first just for coming between your legs and gradually ask for further movement around the outside of your leg. Reward often enough to keep your dog interested and raise your sights a little at a time.

Command:
"Figure eight"; "Through the legs"

Signal:
By placing the dog and yourself in position, saying the command "Figure eight," and pointing in the direction you want the dog to go, you will cue the dog.

Problems:
If your dog will not follow the treat, use your leash as a guide—pass it between your legs and hold it in your right hand so you can lead the dog through and around to the right. Or use a short traffic leash or a tab attached to the dog's collar. Hold it in the same hand as the treat and use it to guide the dog through. Be very gentle and don't ask too much at first. Your dog needs her confidence built up.

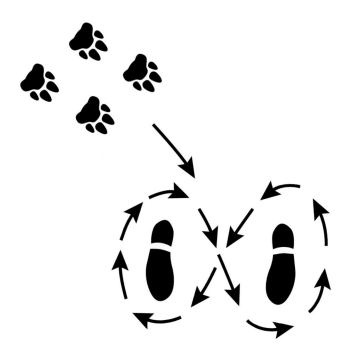

Sasha the Australian Cattle Dog demonstrating Figure eight through the legs.

1. Standing with your legs spread a little wider than shoulder width, have your dog in a Sit behind you.

2. Hold a treat in each hand and lure the dog through your legs, keeping your other hand out of the way.

5. Now pull away the first hand you were using and continue to lure the dog with your other hand.

6. Bring the dog back around the outside of your other leg.

3. Continue to lure the dog back around the outside of your leg.

4. When your dog gets to the back of your leg, bring your other hand through your legs to meet your lure hand.

7. Lure the dog as far as possible behind you, then pull away that hand and use the hand you started with to lure the dog all the way through.

8. Once the dog comes through your legs this time, she's completed the Figure eight.

THE CLICKER

Prerequisites: A clicker. This is a small child's toy that makes a double clicking sound. You can find them at party supply stores or toy stores or novelty shops.

Uses: A dog trained to come to a clicker can be sent from person to person without any audible command or visual signal. This is used often in theater work. In pet therapy work, having the patient click the clicker puts them in control of the dog, which is usually met with great enthusiasm. A clicker can also be used in training any behaviors in this book. Some dogs may learn more quickly with the clicker. Try picking a behavior and training with the clicker to see how the dog does.

Action: If the dog knows a recall (and all dogs should), click the clicker several times, then give your "Come" command or signal. When the dog gets to you, give him a treat. Every time the dog comes to the clicker, he should get a food reward. When the dog is accustomed to the clicker, phase out the command/signal. Just click the clicker once.

The clicker can also be used in teaching behaviors, especially more difficult ones. For example, Bow. If your timing is not good, you may end up rewarding your dog when he is on his way down or before his elbows are on the ground. The clicker can help you by being the bridge between the dog doing the correct action and getting his reward. By clicking the clicker at the exact moment the dog is in the correct position, you let the dog know he's doing the behavior you want. The reward then follows.

Spend a little time for a couple of days just clicking the clicker and rewarding the animal every time you click. When you've started to associate the clicker with food, wait until the dog is distracted and click the clicker. Just as Pavlov rang the bell, you're going to click the clicker. It's easier for some people to click the clicker at the appropriate moment than to tell the dog it's doing a good job.

In this instance, you would say "Bow," do the action it takes to get the dog into position, click the clicker when he's in position, then reward the dog.

Timing: Reward the dog each time she comes to you or does the proper behavior.

Command: Say nothing—click the clicker, or give the command for the behavior.

Signal: None

Problems: If you have a dog who is shy of strangers, he may be reluctant to go to other people when they click. Start with people the dog knows and be sure to give treats every time and lots of praise.

You still have to be sure to use the proper timing with the clicker, rewarding what it is you want.

1. With the clicker and a treat in your hand, wait until your dog gets distracted, click the clicker, and call the dog.

2. Continue to click the clicker as the dog is coming to you.

3. Once he gets to you, reward him. Once he's responding to the clicker, stop using the verbal command and click the clicker less often.

Buster the mixed breed demonstrating how the clicker can be used in training other behaviors.

THE GRAPEVINE

Prerequisites: Figure eight through the legs, Circle left/Circle right are helpful

Uses: A good flexibility exercise. It is also closely related to the working of agility weave poles. But it is simply a charming exercise on its own. As part of your pet therapy entertainment routine, it's sure to be well received.

Action: Have the dog do a few Figure eights through the legs to get warmed up. Now have the dog sitting on your left side with his nose pointing toward you at a 90-degree angle to you. Have a treat in each hand. Step straight forward with your right foot, as though you're walking. Put your left hand behind your back. Lure the dog all the way through your legs with your right hand, then into a half circle so he's facing you again. Now step straight forward with your left leg. Bring your left hand behind your left leg to meet your right hand. Hide your right hand behind your back. Lure the dog all the way through your legs and into a half circle so he's facing you again. Now repeat.

Timing: Be sure to reward and praise enthusiastically the first few times your dog finds her way through your legs and back around. Don't try to take too many steps too soon or you will confuse your dog. Watch for signs of stress—this behavior can be quite confusing to the dog (and you).

Command: "Grapevine"; "Weave"; "In and out"

Signal: By placing the dog and yourself in position, giving the command "Grapevine," and pointing in the direction you want the dog to go, you will cue the dog.

Problems: Make sure you circle the dog far enough out so that when he comes back to face you he's not in the way of your moving leg.

If you are short and your dog is tall, you have a problem! If this is the case, but this behavior really appeals to you, try lifting up your leg so your dog can pass under it before you put it back down. Problems here are likely to be similar to those encountered in Figure eight through the legs. See that behavior earlier in this chapter for suggestions.

1. Standing with your dog sitting facing you at your left, extend your right leg forward as if in mid-stride.

2. With the treat in your right hand, lure the dog between your legs.

3. Be sure the dog comes all the way through so your left leg is free to move.

Dutch the mixed breed demonstrating Grapevine.

4. Lure the dog around in a half circle so he's facing you from the right side.

5. Step forward with your left leg. Bring your left hand forward with its treat to meet your right hand.

6. Hide your right hand behind your back and use your left hand to lure the dog through your legs and into a half circle to face you again.

CHAPTER 9
ATHLETE TURNED ACTOR

Is your dog a bundle of energy? The following behaviors can help burn up some of that fire. Just be sure your dog is not suffering any joint or back problems before beginning any jumping program.

All of these behaviors are variations on a theme. Try one or two or work on them all. If you are going beyond basic obedience or into agility or flyball, your dog will be doing plenty of jumping anyway. These behaviors will offer a little variety.

Always start any jumping behavior at a minimal height. Increase the height gradually. And any time you change the behavior, such as working from jumping through a hoop to jumping through your arms, lower the height back to your starting position. Don't ever be in a hurry with any behavior involving jumping. Mistakes can injure your dog's body and her confidence.

Be careful of working the dog on slick floors. If you will be using jumping in your pet therapy repertoire, find an area that is carpeted or that offers secure footing for the dog.

HOOP JUMP

Prerequisites: Stand, Stay

Uses: Good for maximum exercise in minimum space. Can be quite a flashy performance, especially if you have a large dog and a small hoop. Can be useful for teaching a dog to jump compactly, with feet well tucked up.

Note that you can often find inexpensive hoops in the toy department of discount stores. Some people have been lucky enough to find hoops that are made in sections, so that a section can be removed to make a smaller hoop.

Action: Position the dog in a Stand, Stay to your left or right. Hold the hoop slightly off the ground. Offer a treat on the side of the hoop opposite the dog and encourage the dog through. As the dog gets the idea, slowly raise the hoop. Keep raising it until you reach a height suitable for your dog's jumping efforts. You can create a more impressive show by decorating your hoop or holding it behind your back and having the dog jump back and forth through the hoop.

Timing: Reward the dog immediately after he clears the hoop at first. When you have raised the height, wait to reward him until the dog has collected himself after landing. As always, as your dog gains understanding of the behavior, reward intermittently.

Command: "Hoop"; "Jump"; "Through"

Signal: A sweeping arm motion in the direction the dog will be jumping.

Problems: If the dog will not go through the hoop to get the treat, use your leash to help lead him through, and give plenty of encouragement. Make a big fuss when he does it. If you're having trouble, you can also try throwing one of your dog's favorite toys through the hoop.

1. Start with the dog in a Stand, Stay. Hold the treat through the hoop.

2. Lure her through and give your command. Have her walk through at first.

3. Once she's doing well, start to raise the hoop gradually, asking for a better performance each session.

4. Remember not to move the hoop when the dog is jumping.

5. Reward the dog when she gets to the other side.

Sunday the mixed breed demonstrating Hoop Jump.

JUMP THROUGH YOUR ARMS

Prerequisites: Hoop Jump

Uses: Another flashy behavior that doesn't require any props. It does require trust both on your dog's part and on yours, because the dog will be jumping very close to your face. Some people find this far more impressive than the hoop jump.

Action: Do a couple of Hoop Jumps to warm up. Then kneel down so that the hoop is low and hold it with your arms following the curve of the hoop. At first put your arms only partway around the hoop. Hold it out as far from your body as possible. Keep your head back out of the way. Command your dog through the hoop. If she seems secure with this, move your arms more around the hoop the next time. When you have brought your arms around to form a nearly complete circle, eliminate the hoop.

Timing: Reward the dog as before, as soon as she has completed the jump.

Command: "Hoop"; "Jump"; "Through"

Signal: Forming the hoop with your arms

Problems: Many dogs are reluctant to jump close to your face, and see your arms as somehow more confining than the hoop. They may be hesitant under the new conditions you are presenting. If you have a training partner, he or she can help in coaxing the dog through. If you are on your own, you will just have to proceed slowly with lots of encouragement.

1. Make sure your dog performs the Hoop Jump very reliably. Now you can start wrapping your arms partway around the hoop and give the cue for the dog to jump through.

2. Still holding the hoop, start to make a smaller circle with your arms. Once the dog is doing well, you're ready to move to the next phase.

3. Now remove the hoop and have the dog jump through your arms.

Cubby the Norwich Terrier demonstrating Jumping through the arms.

JUMP OVER LEG/BAR

Prerequisites: Stand Stay, Hoop Jump

Uses: Could fit very nicely in a canine freestyle routine, where handler and dog perform choreography to music. Useful practice for obedience jumping, especially if you have progressed to Utility where there is a bar jump. A flashy behavior sure to impress spectators. Doesn't require any props.

Action: Put the dog in a Stand. Start by using a bar. Hold the bar low and parallel to the ground. Entice the dog over with a treat. Gradually raise the bar. Now put the bar next to your outstretched leg and have the dog jump over it. Practice this several times, then remove the bar. Your own balance will be very important if you are doing Jump over leg.

Timing: Reward as before, as soon as the dog is back on the ground.

Command: "Over"; "Leg"; "Bar"

Signal: Sweep your arm over the leg or bar in the direction the dog will be jumping.

Problems: If the dog tries to go around, put your foot flat against the wall or put a chair against the wall and put your foot on it. If the dog tries to go under, you may be going too high too soon.

1. Start with your dog in a Stand. Hold the treat on the other side of the bar.

2. Give the jump command and have your dog jump over the bar. Reward him on the other side. Gradually move the bar higher.

3. Now that your dog is jumping the bar well, put the bar beside your leg, hold them both up together and ask your dog to jump.

4. When your dog is accustomed to this, remove the bar and have him jump over your leg.

McGee the mixed breed demonstrating Bar Jump.

ALLEY-OOP/HUG

Prerequisites: Sit (for small dogs), Feet Up (for large dogs)

Uses: With small dogs, Alley oop can lead to some flashy behaviors, such as leaping from a platform across open space into the owner's arms. It can also save the owner's back when picking up the dog. For dogs too large to catch in your arms, Feet up can become a heartwarming hug. This is not a hug you would want to use in pet therapy, as the hug recipient will be bearing some of the dog's weight.

Action: For Alley-oop, sit in a low chair. Using encouragement, food, or a toy tucked under your chin, encourage the dog to jump into your lap. *Be sure and catch the dog!* Pet her and love her and give her a treat—make this a positive experience before you put her down. Little by little, straighten up out of the chair. Keep your knees bent slightly to give the dog a push-off platform for getting up into your arms. Always be ready to securely catch the dog. Once she is accomplished at this, you can place her on a platform and ask her to jump to you—stay fairly close at first.

For larger dogs, you ask for a Feet up using your chest or shoulders as the target. Be prepared to bear the dog's weight. To make a really pretty hug, also have the dog do a Head down on your shoulder or chest. Wrap your arms around the dog to return the hug. You can even add a Kiss if you have taught the dog this behavior.

Timing: Be sure to make this an enjoyable behavior—the dog is putting a lot of trust in you. Don't hold a dog in the Hug position if she is not comfortable. Make sure you do hold a small dog comfortably and securely in your arms. Offer treats, praise, whatever will make your dog happy.

Command: "Alley-oop"; "Hug"; "Give us a hug"

Signal: Bring both arms in and tap your chest or thighs.

Problems: Most problems would be caused by the handler—not catching the dog securely or stepping on the back feet of a hugging dog. Don't be concerned that teaching your dog to hug will give her license to jump up on people. This behavior, as all behaviors, should only be accepted on command.

1. While sitting down, start with
the dog in a Sit in front of you.

2. Encourage the dog to jump
into your lap.

3. Give the command "Alley-oop"
as the dog is jumping.

4. Remember to catch the dog
and praise and reward her.

5. Once she's jumping well onto your lap, stand partway up out of your chair, moving closer to a standing position with each session.

6. You always need to keep your legs bent slightly to provide a platform for your dog.

7. Always hold your dog comfortably and securely when she's in your arms.

Touché the Jack Russell Terrier demonstrating Alley-oop.

CHAPTER 10
EXTRAS

Here are a few miscellaneous behaviors before we move on to a brief discussion of how to make the most of what you've learned here. After adding these behaviors to what you've already learned, you will have well over two dozen new tricks in your repertoire.

The first two of these behaviors are related, with Counting a more advanced form of Speak. If you work at it, you can make this so subtle that it truly baffles your spectators. Teaching Whisper makes Say your prayers much more effective—you don't want a dog who *shouts* his prayers, after all.

Kiss is an easy behavior to teach. Your dog probably offers plenty of this on his own. Now you're going to put it on cue. If you participate in pet therapy, you will find this a very well-received talent (though you should always ask permission before having your dog give someone a kiss).

Our final behavior, Say your prayers, fits in quite nicely with the subject of the next chapter, putting a series of behaviors together to tell a story. If you've taught Feet up and Speak, you're close to having this behavior accomplished.

SPEAK/WHISPER

Prerequisites: None

Uses: Part of Say your prayers, and the basis for Counting. A great behavior to have in your act; can be added to almost any storytelling routine you might devise.

Action: A lot of people teach this by waiting until the dog barks and immediately giving their command, even going so far as to set up situations that will set the dog off, such as having a friend ring the doorbell. This will eventually work, but try this instead for faster results: With the leash attached to your dog's buckle collar (not a training collar), tie the dog to a secure object or have someone hold the leash. Stand about four to six feet out of the dog's reach and offer a treat, a ball, or whatever your dog really wants to get to. Make yourself and the object you're using really enticing. Encourage the dog to get the treat or come to you. Most dogs will bark out of frustration. Any sound or any effort toward creating a sound should be rewarded. Ask for a little better performance each time. Add the command/signal to speak.

To teach Whisper, once you have a reliable Speak, put your finger over your lips as if you are shushing someone and very quietly say Speak. Continue to ask for the behavior until the dog responds with a halfhearted sort of bark. Eventually switch the word "Speak" to "Whisper."

Timing: When teaching Speak, as soon as the dog barks or makes any sound, throw the treat or toy to the dog. Remember, lots of praise. It probably won't take very long for your dog to catch on to this. When he seems to understand, still have him tied or held but move closer and give your command and/or signal and see if he responds to the command. If you do not get a bark, move back out to where the dog can't reach you and continue to entice him with your treat.

Command: "Speak"; "Bark"

Signal: Hold your hand up next to your head with index finger outstretched and shake it.

Problems: *Never* reward a dog for barking if you have not cued him. You do not want to create a noisy monster.

Some dogs just do not offer a lot of barking. If you have one of these quiet types, remember in the beginning to reward any whine or snort and try to work up to a lusty bark. Or try the alternate method mentioned first under "Action."

1. Have someone hold your dog on a leash or tie the leash to a secure object.

2. Entice the dog with either food, a toy, or by calling her from about four to six feet away. You may have to act goofy and maybe even play bow to your dog.

3. Continue to excite the dog until she either whines, whimpers, or speaks. Immediately reward the dog.

4. Keep repeating this sequence
and add the command "Speak."

5. Once she performs the
behavior readily, have her
sit and give the signal and
command to speak.

6. After you have Speak well in hand, you can try "Whisper," using a "shush" signal.

Tessa the Dalmatian demonstrating Speak.

COUNT/ANSWER QUESTIONS

Prerequisites: Speak

Uses: With some extra work, you can turn your dog into an apparent math wizard, taking problems in arithmetic from the audience and having the dog answer them. Or you can do a little vaudeville turn with your dog answering stupid questions.

Action: You've taught the dog to bark on cue, now you'll teach him to stop on cue. Start by holding your hand up and giving the Speak cue. Have the dog bark once, lower your hand, and reward the dog. Now do the same thing, but hold up two fingers as you signal and have your dog bark twice before lowering your hand and rewarding. Do not reward the dog if he continues to bark after you put your hand down. Do the same thing for three, four, five, and so on.

In the beginning you may have to add more body language to cue the dog. Associate the word "Speak" with "How many fingers am I holding up?" until you no longer have to say "Speak." Or make the association with your silly question, such as "What did the dog say when he sat on the sandpaper?" ("Ruff," of course.)

Now you're ready for an audience. Do your vaudeville schtick, or, if you are counting, have someone pick a number between one and five. Hold up the appropriate number of fingers. Ask the dog, "How many fingers am I holding up?" Subtly lower your hand after your dog has reached the appropriate number of barks. Wait a beat, then reward your dog with a treat. The more subtle you can be with your cues, the more amazed your audience will be.

Timing: If you really want this act to be impressive, your cuing and timing are everything. Many dogs enjoy barking and will not always wait for your "Speak" signal once they know how the act works. It will help if you do not make eye contact with the dog until you are ready for his answer. You may also have to remove the cue slightly before your dog actually gives the last bark to get him to stop on time. A good way to get your dog to stop on cue is to learn to toss a treat with your hand at your side away from your audience so it is unobtrusive.

Command: "How many fingers am I holding up?" or "What did the dog say when he sat on the sandpaper?"

Signal: Appropriate number of fingers or body cue or facial cue. You want to work to make your cue as subtle as possible.

Problems: If your dog barks enthusiastically, make sure that you cue him at the end of your question. For instance, have him sit in front of you, show him you have a treat, close it up in your hand, then do not look at the dog as you say, "What did the dog say when he sat . . ." Now look at him and give your subtle cue as you finish ". . . on the sandpaper." If your dog takes a lot of cuing, you will want to start cuing him much earlier. You need to get your timing down so that the bark comes in the correct place and your audience doesn't realize that you are cuing the dog.

Tessa the Dalmatian demonstrating Counting. Remember to be expressive with your body when cuing the dog.

KISS

Prerequisites: None

Uses: Wonderful for pet therapy or for dogs involved in schoolroom pet education classes. Equally useful in your everyday activities, such as when encountering children while walking in the park.

Action: You can practice this on yourself if you have to, but it is better to have helpers right from the beginning—you will want your dog to kiss anyone you indicate, not just you.

Have some meat-flavored baby food on hand. Put some of the baby food on your helper's cheek. Have the helper squat or kneel to be within easy reach of the dog. Take your dog up to the helper and say "Kiss" while maneuvering the dog toward the baby food. If the dog does not begin licking on her own, point toward the baby food with your finger and encourage her to lick it. If your dog does not seem fond of the baby food, try a different flavor or switch to peanut butter or squeeze cheese.

Make sure you are targeting the dog to the cheek with the food motivator. Some people do not like a dog kissing them on the mouth. Once the dog has licked the baby food off, have him return to you and give him a treat so he will associate kissing with getting a treat from you.

Once your dog seems to have the idea, stop walking up to the helper and stop using the baby food. Stay a little distance away and send the dog. The dog must go give a kiss and return to you for his reward. Be sure to use as many different helpers as possible—men and women, young and old, tall and short.

Timing: The baby food is the dog's reward, but you should remember to praise, especially if your dog is hesitant.

Command: "Kiss"; "Go kiss"

Signal: Sweep your arm in the direction of the person while giving your command.

Problems: Shy dogs will likely have problems with this behavior, but it can also be a good confidence builder. Start with people the dog knows and accepts and make your practices short and positive. Instruct your helpers not to look at the dog and to keep still.

1. In teaching Kiss, place a small amount of whatever food reward you're using on the person's cheek.

2. Point to where the food reward is and give the command "Kiss."

3. Once the dog is doing well, stop using food on the helper's face, and just give your command "Kiss." Once the dog has kissed the person, have her return to you for the treat.

SAY YOUR PRAYERS/PRAY

Prerequisites: Feet Up, Whisper

Uses:
A good behavior as part of storytelling. Also a nice stretching exercise for the neck and back. Both young and old spectators are likely to react with "ahs."

Action:
Stand or kneel, depending on your dog's size. With your dog standing, hold your nonactive arm (your left if you're right-handed) out parallel to the ground. Have the dog do Feet up on the outside of your arm. Do this for several sessions so your dog is comfortable with this.

Now have your dog do Feet up on your arm, then take your treat and offer it under your extended arm to the dog, making the dog duck her head between her paws to get the treat. Give your command "Pray" and immediately reward the dog. Practice this for several sessions. Occasionally practice with the dog's feet up on a bar or an open-backed chair.

When the dog seems to be catching on, omit the "Feet up" command. Just offer your arm and give your "Pray" command. Once your dog is comfortable with this, give your command "Whisper" while your dog is in the pray position. Reward. Practice this for several sessions. As your release command, say "Amen."

Timing:
At first, reward the dog for each behavior you ask for—"Feet up," "Pray," "Whisper." As you become more accomplished at this, the dog has to perform the entire sequence and hold her position for several seconds before being rewarded. When you have really got it all together, the dog must actually say her prayers before being rewarded.

Command:
"Say your prayers"; "Pray"

Signal:
Extend your arm or point to some other chosen target as you give your command.

Problems:
Dogs often take one paw off your arm as they try to tuck their head or may even jump off completely. Take it slow and be patient. You can try having your dog start from a Sit and see if that works better for you.

1. Start with the dog in a Stand with your arm extended.

2. Give your dog the command "Feet up" on your arm. Work on this for several sessions until your dog feels comfortable doing the behavior.

3. Now with the dog in the Feet up position on your arm, use a treat to lure the dog's head down through her front legs and give the command "Pray."

Kelly the mixed breed demonstrating Say your prayers.

CHAPTER 11
THE PLOT LINE

You and your dog have now learned a whole variety of exciting new behaviors. You're probably enjoying showing them off. Your audience is probably deeply impressed. But you can do more.

When you teach a complicated behavior or combine behaviors into a storytelling sequence, you break it down into separate pieces, train each one, and then put them together. This is called chaining. In teaching Say your prayers, you chain several behaviors together to create a new behavior. Now we're going to chain behaviors to tell a story.

Choose five or six behaviors your dog does well. Now, think of how you can put those behaviors together to tell a story.

Say, for example, your dog does well at speaking, playing dead, crawling, and taking a bow. Watch how these behaviors combine to tell a war story.

We need a mission. How about a member of the underground bringing critical information back from the front? And of course there has to be a bad guy. Now for some details.

Every good dog should say his prayers before going off to war. You never know if you're coming back. His superior officer then orders him to the front to retrieve critical information from an underground informant.

Canine special agent makes his rendezvous with his contact and receives the critical information. The informant then points the canine special agent back to base camp. While hurrying back, the brave canine special agent encounters a bad guy. He's shot and left for dead. But he was only wounded, and manages to drag himself in a painful crawl back to his superior officer. With his last breath, he's able to bark out the critical information necessary to save the troops. But, alas, the effort was too much for him and he collapses. But don't worry—canine special agent recuperated in a rehabilitation hospital and is doing just fine.

Okay, maybe it's silly. But you can come up with your own story. Whatever story you're using, it's important that people understand what's going on or it might not make much sense. So deliver a little spiel before the action, something like this:

"Canine special agent is a member of the underground during World War II. His mission is to reach a contact across enemy lines and bring back critical information. He stands a good chance of being shot, but he'll do his best to make it back. And because the mission is so dangerous, he'll say a prayer before he goes."

One place to get ideas from is your television. Dogs are very popular in advertising and film, and you'll probably see at least one in any given series of commercial breaks or as a regular on a TV show. If you see a dog doing something you'd like to train your dog to do, think about how the behavior might have been accomplished.

We hope that you have received great enjoyment from this book and that you and your dog will bond even more closely through training these behaviors. Most dogs are show-offs at heart, and enjoy being in the spotlight. Share your dog's new abilities so everyone can enjoy them.

GLOSSARY

Agility: an organized dog sport in which dogs negotiate a course comprised of jumps, tunnels, and other obstacles

Bait bag: a small pouch attached to a belt or waistband for holding treats

Bar jump: a jump used in the Utility division of obedience competition, consisting of a bar supported on stanchions

Bending: a flexibility exercise in which the dog is encouraged to flex his or her spine; also a term for performance of the agility weave poles

Canine freestyle: an organized dog sport in which dog and handler perform a choreographed routine to music, using obedience, trick training, jumping, etc.

Chaining: combining small components of a behavior into a whole performance, or combining separate behaviors into a sequence

Clicker training: training using a small noisemaker as a cue to the dog; the dog is taught to associate the sound with a food reward, and the clicker is then clicked at the precise moment that the dog is performing some desired behavior

Conformation: an organized dog sport in which dogs are judged on their physical makeup against a written standard of perfection for their breed

Correction training: traditional training method that uses a training collar and physical manipulation to put the dog in the desired position, with corrections delivered as jerks on the collar for incorrect behavior

Crawl tunnel: an obstacle in agility, which the dog must crawl under

Drives: a dog's motivational components; a dog chasing a ball is in prey drive, imitating the chasing of prey; a dog drooling over the meatloaf on the kitchen counter is in food drive

Finish: an exercise in formal obedience, where the dog moves from sitting in front of the handler to sitting at the handler's left side

Flyball: an organized dog sport in which teams of dogs relay race over a series of hurdles, catch a ball propelled out of a box, and return over the hurdles

Food training: training using food both as a lure and as a reward

Go-out: an exercise in Utility obedience, in which the dog must move from alongside the handler at one side of the ring to cross the ring and, when commanded, turn to face the handler and sit

Group long down: an exercise in Novice and Open obedience, in which a group of dogs must maintain a down for three minutes with their handlers standing across the ring (Novice), or for five minutes with the handlers out of sight (Open)

Heeling: an exercise in all levels of obedience, in which the dog must maintain a position at the handler's left side while walking or trotting

Intermittent reward: a reward offered sporadically (an example of a powerful intermittent reward in the context of human experience is the payoff from a slot machine—this expected payoff can keep a person gambling)

Long sit: an exercise in Novice and Open obedience, in which a group of dogs must maintain a sit for one minute with their handlers standing across the ring (Novice) or for three minutes with their handlers out of sight (Open)

Lure: food or a toy used as an enticement to get a dog to move into the desired position

Negative reinforcers: punishment or anything the dog will strive to avoid

Novice: the beginning level of formal obedience, in which the dog must heel, stand, come when called, and perform a sit stay (long sit) and down stay (group long down)

Obedience: an organized dog sport in which dogs perform a series of exercises including heeling, standing, coming when called, and staying in a sit and down; more advanced levels include retrieving and off-leash work

Open: the second level of formal obedience, in which the dog must heel off-leash, retrieve a dumbbell over a jump, do a down in the middle of a recall, and stay in a sit and down with their handler out of sight

Pet therapy: bringing dogs to visit those in hospitals or convalescent hospitals in order to cheer them up

Play bow: a natural behavior, in which the dog lowers his front end to the ground with his rear in the air, used to induce another dog (or human) to play

Pretraining: work done before an acting assignment in order to have the dog perform some difficult piece of behavior specifically requested

Prey drive: a basic motivation calling on the dog's hunting instinct; herding dogs exhibit a strong prey drive but stop short of actually making the "kill"

Puppy push-ups: an aerobic exercise in which the dog is commanded to sit, down, sit, down repeatedly

Reach: the extension of the dog's forelegs out in front of the dog when moving, especially at a trot

Recall: the "Come" command, wherein the dog will stop whatever he or she is doing and return to the handler

School visit programs: educational programs in which an owner brings a dog to school and discusses care and training and how to behave around dogs

Search and rescue: activities of trained dog/handler teams using the dog's scenting abilities to find lost people or those trapped in disaster areas

Shaping: developing a behavior by accepting a small step toward the behavior at first and gradually demanding performance closer to the full behavior

Stack: in the conformation ring, the display of the dog in a standing position, in which the dog's feet must be carefully placed to show the dog off to best advantage

Tab: a short, three- to five-inch piece of leather or nylon that can be attached to the dog's collar to offer a convenient handle for correcting or controlling the dog

Traffic leash: a short, typically three-foot leash, meant to keep the dog under close control

Training collar: also called a slip collar or choke collar, a collar that tightens about the dog's neck when pressure is applied through the leash

Utility: the highest level of obedience, in which the dog must perform scent discrimination exercises (e.g., choosing a dumbbell that the owner has handled), silent exercises (with signals only), and the go-out, among others

Weave poles: an agility obstacle, which the dog performs by zig-zagging through a series of poles spaced along a line

Skill	Date Started Training	Number of Practice Sessions (ЖНГ, etc.)	Problems Encountered	Solutions Tried	Got Best Results From	Date Dog Understood	Can Work from a Distance Of	Use in Story Line or Routine
Wave/ High Five								
Sit Up/Beg								
Bang/ Play Dead								
Where's Your Nose?								
Head Down/ Head Up								
On Your Side								

Skill	Date Started Training	Number of Practice Sessions (JHT, etc.)	Problems Encountered	Solutions Tried	Got Best Results From	Date Dog Understood	Can Work from a Distance Of	Use in Story Line or Routine
Crawl								
Roll Over								
Feet Up								
Put 'Em Up/ Walk								
Take a Bow								
Cirle Left/ Right								

Skill	Date Started Training	Number of Practice Sessions (JHT, etc.)	Problems Encountered	Solutions Tried	Got Best Results From	Date Dog Understood	Can Work from a Distance Of	Use in Story Line or Routine
Back Up								
Figure Eight								
The Clicker								
The Grapevine								
Hoop Jump								
Jump Through Arms								

Skill	Date Started Training	Number of Practice Sessions (JHT, etc.)	Problems Encountered	Solutions Tried	Got Best Results From	Date Dog Understood	Can Work from a Distance Of	Use in Story Line or Routine
Jump Over Leg/Bar								
Alley-Oop/ Hug								
Speak/ Whisper								
Count/ Answer Questions								
Kiss								
Say Your Prayers/Pray								